# DISCOVERING
# SHARKS and RAYS

**By**
**Nancy Field**

Illustrated by Michael Maydak

Computer Designer Betsy True
With research contributions from Wil Burns

Text copyright © 2003 Nancy Field
Artwork copyright © 2003 Michael Maydak
Second Printing 2012

Tracking Label Book: UG0712-2WIUS
Tracking Label Stickers: WP0612-1WIUS

ISBN 10: 0-941042-33-2
ISBN 13: 978-0-941042-33-8

*Printed in the USA on Recycled Paper*

# Have You Ever Wondered?

Beep beep. Beep… beep …beep.
SHARK ALERT! SHARK ALERT!

The research boat quickly changes course but not to turn and run! Instead, it heads straight for the churning water where a school of lemon sharks is feeding. The scientists on board have been cruising along the coast, hoping to hear the beeping sound that comes from tags that were put on several sharks a few weeks ago.

The shark biologists and their young research assistants plan to put tiny transponders on other sharks. They will measure them and take blood samples. The information they collect may later be used to help the sharks.

Scientists have to follow sharks out into the ocean to learn their secrets. They cannot learn all they need to know from sharks in an aquarium. They cannot, for example, study hunting behavior or migration routes. Capturing sharks has to be done carefully because some **species** (kinds) get so stressed out during the struggle that they die. Captive sharks need moving water to help them breathe. They tend to be sensitive to electrical levels in the water in a tank. Some cannot survive in a tank with metal frames around windows or steel bars.

Studying sharks is an interesting job—and it isn't as dangerous as you might think. The average person has more chance of being hit by lightening than of being bitten by a shark. On the other hand, if you are a fish, you have a good reason to fear sharks. Most sharks are carnivores. Many are meat eaters—or, in their case, fish eaters.

Dive in and surf this book. Discover the world of sharks and rays.

Are sharks like other fish?
*See pages 4-5*

Where do sharks and rays live?
*See pages 6, 22-27*

Are sharks and rays related?
*See page 6*

What are shark teeth like?
*See page 15*

Is it natural for one kind of animal to eat another?
*See pages 12-13*

Do sharks kill people?
*See pages 9 and 33*

**Southern Stingray**

**Lemon Shark**

Is it safe
to get in
the water with
a shark?
*See page 5*

How are
sharks and rays
valuable to
people?
*See pages
10 and 11*

How do you
tag a shark?
*See page 36*

What are
people doing
to help sharks?
*See pages
38 and 39*

Can you
survive as a
shark or ray?
*Play the game
on pages
29-31*

Is
it possible to
be safe in shark
country?
*See page 33*

Do
sharks have
any serious
problems?
*See page 32
and play the game
on pages
29-31*

Why do
biologists study
sharks and rays?
What do they want
to find out?
*See page 34*

Are pups
born live or
from eggs?
*See page
26*

**Nurse Shark**

# Fishy Questions

**Sam Gruber**
*Shark Biologist*
*Florida*

These scientists have captured a shark—or is it some other kind of fish? All sharks are fish, but not all fish are sharks! So how do you tell if a fish is a shark? The most important clue lies in the skeleton. A shark's skeleton is made of **cartilage**. Cartilage is a tough rubbery material. (We have cartilage in our noses and ears.) True fish, such as salmon and goldfish, have skeletons made of bone. They are called "bony fish."

Like us, sharks breathe oxygen. We get oxygen from the air around us. Sharks get their oxygen from the water. Water flows through their mouths and passes out over the gills.

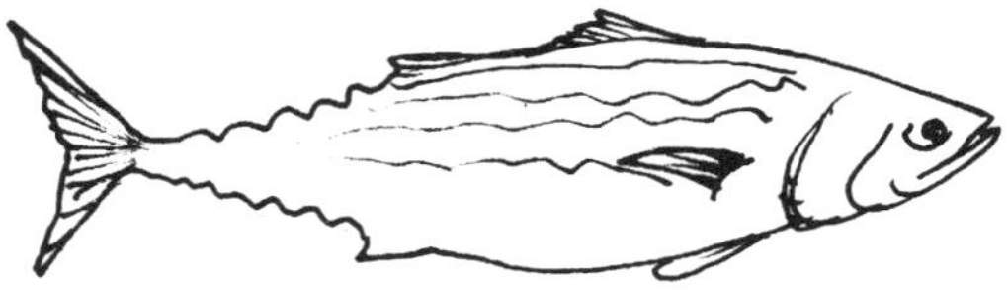

You don't have to examine the skeleton to tell a shark from other fish. The gills provide clue. Sharks have several gill slits, while fish have one bony flap or gill cover.

What are gills for?

A. _____

B. _____

**Label these animals: shark or bony fish?**

Answers on last page

4

Doctor Sam Gruber is from the University of Miami in Florida. He runs a "Shark Lab" in the Bimini Islands in the Bahamas. He is showing how to hold a young lemon shark. He will put it in the holding pen where it will stay for several days until his work is complete. Then it will be released.

Most sharks are not dangerous to humans. Biologists sometimes work with them in the water.

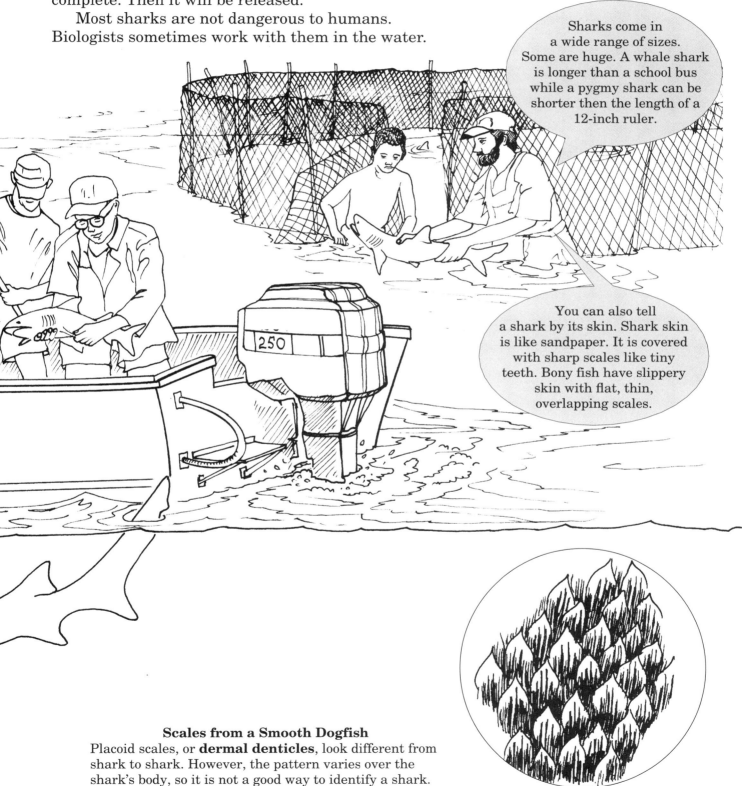

Sharks come in a wide range of sizes. Some are huge. A whale shark is longer than a school bus while a pygmy shark can be shorter then the length of a 12-inch ruler.

You can also tell a shark by its skin. Shark skin is like sandpaper. It is covered with sharp scales like tiny teeth. Bony fish have slippery skin with flat, thin, overlapping scales.

**Scales from a Smooth Dogfish**
Placoid scales, or **dermal denticles**, look different from shark to shark. However, the pattern varies over the shark's body, so it is not a good way to identify a shark.

# Meet the Relatives

*Meri, a shark biologist from Australia*

Sharks and rays have been around in one form or another for more than 400 million years. They are a primitive, but successful, form of fish. Scientists often refer to them as **elasmobranchs**.

Elasmobranchs belong to a class of fish called **Chondrichthyes**, with skeletons made of cartilage. Although they are all in the same class, they are not all alike. Some have hammer-shaped heads, some are as flat as pancakes, and some resemble ghosts! This class includes:

1. Sharks, also known as **selachians**;
2. Rays and skates, also known as **batoids**;
3. Ghostsharks and ratfishes, also known as **chimaeras**.

*Here Meri and her assistant capture small sharks using a seine net in shallow water. They will take the live sharks back to an indoor lab to study.*

Sharks mostly have submarine or cigar-shaped bodies. They have from 5 to 7 gill slits on the side of the body. There are about 350 species of selachians.

**Sharpnose Sevengill Shark**

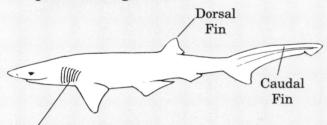

Dorsal Fin

Caudal Fin

Seven gill slits on each side of its head. (Most sharks only have 5 gill slits.)

The lemon shark has two equal-sized dorsal fins and 5 gill slits. Draw a lemon shark (see page 3).

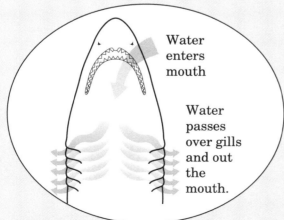

Water enters mouth

Water passes over gills and out the mouth.

Water flows through the mouth and over the gills. As water passes over the very thin skin of the gills, oxygen moves from the water into the shark's blood.

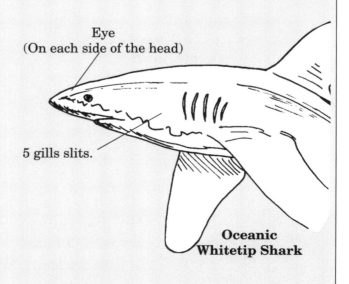

Eye (On each side of the head)

5 gills slits.

**Oceanic Whitetip Shark**

Think of rays as winged sharks. They have pancake-shaped bodies with two eyes on top of the head. They cannot see below themselves. The mouth is on the bottom surface of the body and so are the 5 to 6 pairs of gill slits. The pectoral fins are attached to the back of the skull and are greatly enlarged to form the body disk. The tail is reduced in size and is not used for swimming.

There are over 500 species of batoids. The group includes stingrays, electric rays, skates, guitarfish, and sawfish. The largest is the manta ray, which reaches over 22 feet long (6.7 meters).

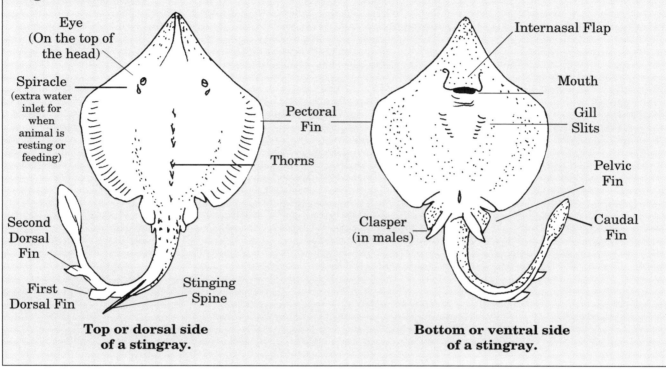

**Top or dorsal side of a stingray.**

**Bottom or ventral side of a stingray.**

**Chimaeras** have upper jaws attached to the skull. They are called ghostfish because of their color and ghost-like appearance. They have one gill opening. They have largely naked skin with no scales. There are more than 38 species of ghost sharks.

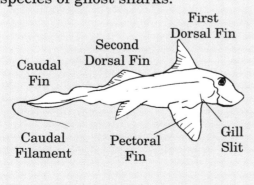

*Back in the lab, Meri studies the pit organs to discover how many there are, and to learn more about what sharks can sense with their pit organs. Live sharks will later be released back into the wild.*

# Where is Home?

Sharks are found in all oceans. They can be found in the depths of the sea, as deep as 13,000 feet (4 km), but most live close to shore because that is where food is plentiful. Most species prefer the warmer waters of temperate, subtropical, or tropical oceans, though some do inhabit polar waters. A few species occur in fresh water.

Some sharks migrate, making a seasonal journey to cooler waters in the summer and warmer waters in winter. Migratory patterns may also tie in with where the pups are born (nursery areas) or with the food supply.

Take a look at where some sharks live.

| **Sharks and Rays** | | **Areas of World** | | | |
|---|---|---|---|---|---|
| **Mark the areas where each kind is found.** | | Tropical<br>*Color light orange* | Subtropical<br>*Color yellow* | Temperate<br>*Color light green* | Polar<br>*Color light blue* |
| Whale Shark | | | | | |
| Great White Shark | | | | | |
| Scalloped Hammerhead | | | | | |
| Mako Shark | | | | | |
| Southern Stingray | | | | | |
| Porbeagle Shark | | | | | |
| Salmon Shark | | | | | |
| Greenland Shark | | | | | |

Answers on last page

# Shark Tales

Why don't some people like sharks?

We don't all think alike. Through the centuries some people have respected them. Others have feared them.

Over 2300 years ago, the Greek philosopher Aristotle knew electric rays could shock and overpower their prey.

Pacific Islanders honored and worshiped sharks. They believed dead family members returned as sharks to help protect the living and the ocean reefs.

The people of the Solomon Islands made carvings of sea spirits with shark heads to look out for them while at sea.

Sharks such as the tiger, bull and white shark sometimes attack and kill people.

Poisonous stingrays can also kill. The stingray spine has been used to make weapons.

Movies often make sharks look evil...

doing things they don't really do.

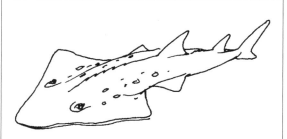

Mostly, sharks and rays are not a danger to humans.

The more we learn about sharks and their place in the ocean, the more we appreciate them and the less we fear them.

Do you want the job?

**Press Agent Wanted**

9

# Shark Uses

**SKIN**

In earlier days, shark parts met numerous different needs. Today, many products are made with other materials.

**Shagreen**
*dried, untanned skin*

- used like sandpaper
- wrapped around handles of swords to keep hands from slipping

**Squalene**
- used in medicines
- used for anticoagulants to keep human blood moving freely.

**LIVER**

Squalene

Lubricant

Soap

Cosmetics

Paint

**CARTILAGE**

Biochemicals

Medicines

**TEETH and JAWS**

Clubs and Implements

Shark Tooth Knife

Necklace

**FINS**

SHARK FIN Soup

**FLESH**

Fertilizer

Fish Portion of Fish and Chips

Fish Meal

*Nancy Field, author*

*Marie Gruber, shark lab*

Respect sharks.
Be careful.
Harvest wisely.

**GALL BLADDER**

Acne Treatment

Acne

Acne

Shark Steaks

10

Sharks have an important role in the overall health of the ocean. They also play a role in our lives in ways that may surprise you. Their bodies are turned into fertilizer and their teeth into jewelry. Their liver provides vitamins and their eyes can be used for cornea transplants. We make medicines from their cartilage. Sharks are naturally resistant to cancer. Scientists are studying this trait, hoping to find a cure for cancer. People eat shark meat.

People also make soup from shark fins. Recently, this dish has become so popular in some countries that sharks are being killed for their fins alone. The rest of the shark is thrown away. Sharks cannot survive this pressure and many species are now at risk.

We look on sharks and rays as a **resource**—something out there for us to use. But demand for shark products is greater than the supply. Sharks are being overfished. People cannot agree what to do. Some want laws that control the use of sharks; others want to keep fishing them.

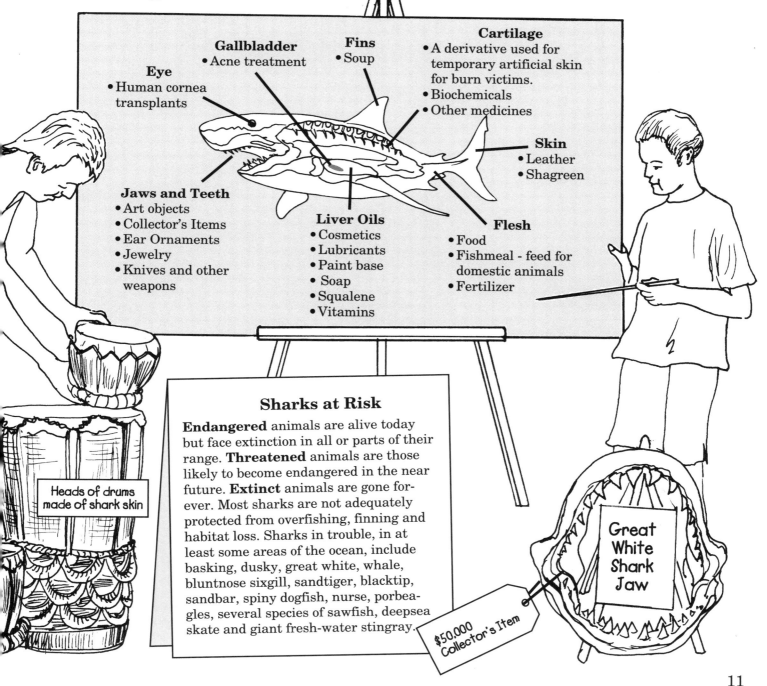

**Gallbladder**
• Acne treatment

**Eye**
• Human cornea transplants

**Fins**
• Soup

**Cartilage**
• A derivative used for temporary artificial skin for burn victims.
• Biochemicals
• Other medicines

**Skin**
• Leather
• Shagreen

**Jaws and Teeth**
• Art objects
• Collector's Items
• Ear Ornaments
• Jewelry
• Knives and other weapons

**Liver Oils**
• Cosmetics
• Lubricants
• Paint base
• Soap
• Squalene
• Vitamins

**Flesh**
• Food
• Fishmeal - feed for domestic animals
• Fertilizer

Heads of drums made of shark skin

### Sharks at Risk

**Endangered** animals are alive today but face extinction in all or parts of their range. **Threatened** animals are those likely to become endangered in the near future. **Extinct** animals are gone forever. Most sharks are not adequately protected from overfishing, finning and habitat loss. Sharks in trouble, in at least some areas of the ocean, include basking, dusky, great white, whale, bluntnose sixgill, sandtiger, blacktip, sandbar, spiny dogfish, nurse, porbeagles, several species of sawfish, deepsea skate and giant fresh-water stingray.

$50,000 Collector's Item

Great White Shark Jaw

# Ocean Hunters

Sharks are probably feared because so many of them are **predators**. Predators are animals that hunt and feed on other animals called **prey**.

Sharks are as important to their marine community as lions are to the African plain. Like lions, they are the top, or **apex** predator in their own environment

Predators play an important role. They are part of nature's balancing act. The pictures show how predators and prey balance each other.

If an apex predator is removed, its loss affects the whole food web.

**When Sharks Are Around**

Sharks like to eat octopuses. Octopuses like to eat crab. When sharks eat some octopuses, then crabs have a better chance to survive. A balance is reached between the octopuses and sharks, and crabs. Without sharks, there are more octopuses and fewer crabs for us to catch in crab pots. Crab is a popular food at home and in restaurants.

# When Sharks Aren't Around

Here, most of the sharks have disappeared, perhaps due to humans killing them. The number of octopuses has grown and they have eaten most of the crabs. There are fewer for people to eat. The balance has been upset.

## Links in Food Chain

It is natural for one thing to eat another. It starts when green plants get energy from the sun.

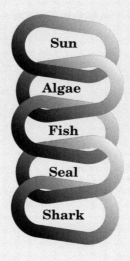

Sun

Algae

Fish

Seal

Shark

In nature, many food chains link together or overlap, making a **food web**. If something happens to one link or chain in the food web, all life may be affected. Starting with the food chain above, can you add more animals and plants to make a food web?

## Are Predators Cruel and Wicked?

A shark eating a seal is no different than a human cutting into a steak. Both are predators. Neither is "mean or bad." They eat to live.

# Designed for the Job

What is a shark's job? Sharks swim through ocean waters looking for food to eat. In the process, they help keep a balance of life in the seas. How many things can you find that make this white shark good at the job of a predator catching its prey?

The form or shape of the animal and its parts are often related to the use or function. Look at the form of the shark and the different parts. Does the shape or form help it do its job? Think about it the other way too. Does the job, perhaps, help determine the shape of the part?

**Eyes** A shark's eyes are very sensitive in dim light, especially in deep water. The lens is seven times more powerful than the lens in our eyes. Some sharks can even see colors when the light is bright and the water is clear.

**Brain and Nose** The sense of smell is important for finding prey. A shark's sense of smell is so good, it has sometimes been called a "swimming nose."

**Lateral Line** A shark has a tube running along each side of the body and beneath the skin. The line also extends over parts of the head. Tiny openings in the line sense movements in the water. This helps the shark find food and other objects.

**Ears** A shark has a keen sense of hearing. Like other fish, it has inner ears in the side of the head behind the eyes. There is a small duct opening to the water. A shark can hear prey in the water over 1/4 mile (about 2/5 km) away.

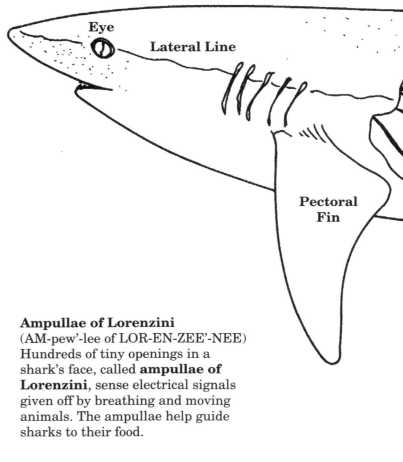

**Ampullae of Lorenzini** (AM-pew'-lee of LOR-EN-ZEE'-NEE) Hundreds of tiny openings in a shark's face, called **ampullae of Lorenzini**, sense electrical signals given off by breathing and moving animals. The ampullae help guide sharks to their food.

**Teeth** Teeth are tools or weapons that are used to get and hold onto food. When a shark bites something hard, a tooth may be lost. Fortunately, there are several rows of teeth. Well developed, upright teeth are in the front. Several inner rows of teeth in various stages of development are folded downward. When teeth in the front fall out, the ones just behind them move up into position and take their place. Sharks are always growing a new set!

A streamlined body is good for moving through water. A rounded body, tapering at both ends reduces drag and requires less energy. Speed and endurance help a shark catch dinner. Some sharks can swim up to 40 miles (64 km) per hour. Most of the shark's swimming power comes from the **caudal** or **tail** fin. As the tail fin moves back and fourth, it propels the shark forward. At the same time, the fin moves upwards and the head points down. The overall effect is forward and downward motion. The **pectoral fins** act like airplane wings. Their shape lets water flow over them and lifts the shark up. This compensates for the downward motion caused by the caudal fin. The **dorsal fins** on the shark's back help keep it upright and steady in the water.

**Pit Organs** Pit organs are tiny pockets in the skin with sensory hair inside them. They are scattered over the body and are guarded by pairs of scales. Pit organs belong to the lateral line system, which senses water motion. The role of these sensory organs in the behavior of sharks is still quite mysterious. In some sharks, they seem to help detect the current direction.

Most fish have a balloon-like organ called a **swim bladder**. By controlling gases within the bladder, fish can float at different depths. This is called **neutral buoyancy**. Sharks don't need swim bladders because of their light skeletons, liver oils, and the design of their bodies.

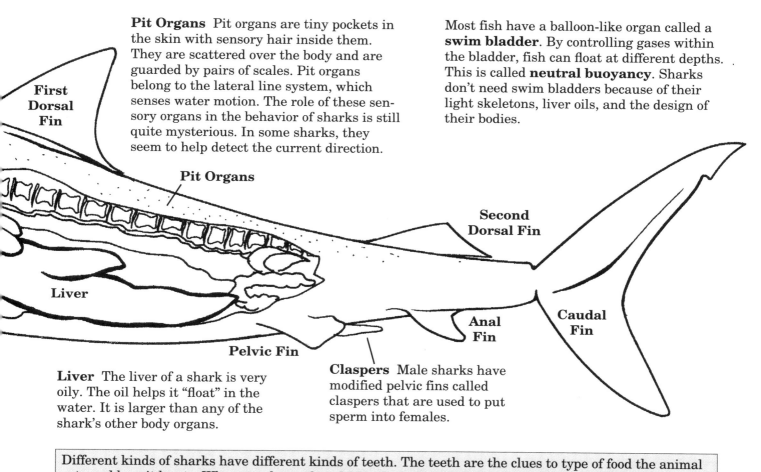

First Dorsal Fin

Pit Organs

Second Dorsal Fin

Liver

Caudal Fin

Anal Fin

Pelvic Fin

**Liver** The liver of a shark is very oily. The oil helps it "float" in the water. It is larger than any of the shark's other body organs.

**Claspers** Male sharks have modified pelvic fins called claspers that are used to put sperm into females.

Different kinds of sharks have different kinds of teeth. The teeth are the clues to type of food the animal eats and how it hunts. Whose teeth are these? **Match the teeth below with the correct shark**.

A. Mako sharks stab and hold slippery prey which is then swallowed whole.

B. Port Jackson sharks, are known as oyster crushers.

C. Tiger sharks cut through bodies like sea turtles.

____1. Large crushing molars at the rear of jaw are used by bottom dwelling sharks to crush hard shells of crustaceans or shrimp-like animals from the ocean bottom.

____2. Sharp, triangular shaped teeth with serrated edges, like a saw, are used for seizing and cutting. Large prey is torn into chunks before eaten.

____3. Long, thin teeth help grab and hold prey which is usually swallowed whole.

# What's for Dinner?

Sharks and rays are hungry animals. What they eat depends on the season and where they live and travel. It is also related to the type of teeth they have. Their food can range from crabs and turtles to dolphins and whales. Some have a favorite food. Horn sharks like sea urchins, blue sharks love squid, and hammerheads prefer stingrays. Some sharks dine on very strange food. Tiger sharks have been called the "garbage cans of the sea." Food found in their stomachs includes tin cans, plastic bags, plastic bottles, a chunk of dog, a pumpkin, a small goat, a tennis shoe, a perfume bottle, and a license plate.

Sharks have different ways of finding and catching their prey. Some have a strong sense of smell. Once the shark detects an odor, it follows it to its source. Electric rays shock their prey. They also use the electrical discharge for defense. The prey have several ways to protect themselves and to escape from hungry sharks. **Unscramble the words below each animal and discover a method of protection**.

Answers on last page

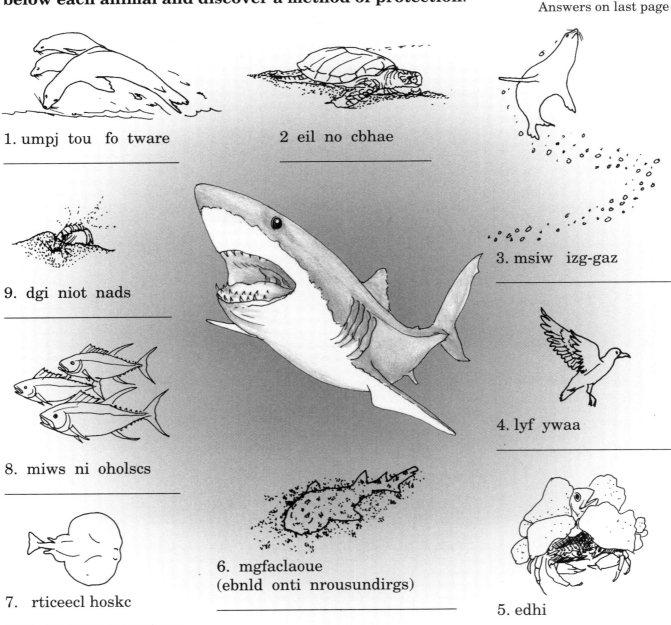

1. umpj tou  fo tware

2 eil no cbhae

3. msiw  izg-gaz

9. dgi niot nads

4. lyf  ywaa

8. miws  ni  oholscs

6.  mgfaclaoue
   (ebnld  onti  nrousundirgs)

7.  rticeecl  hoskc

5. edhi

# An Ocean Mobile

The ocean world is like a mobile. A mobile is made up of several objects hanging by strings. Each object's weight keeps the entire mobile in balance. Take away one piece and the balance is upset. This is also true in the ocean. If some part, such as sharks, is removed, the balance is upset.

Animals and plants that share the same environment interact with each other and the nonliving parts of their surroundings. They form an **ecosystem**. Sharks, rays, turtles, sea lions, fish, crabs, and worms are all important parts of an ocean ecosystem.

To make your own ocean mobile, cut out these images. You might want to laminate the pieces to make them stiff. Or make a copy or each image and cut out a piece of cardboard to put in between the two colored pictures. Matching the letters, assemble your mobile as shown on the diagram on the answer page. You'll need strong thread, fine string or dental floss and two sticks 12-18 inches long. Tie or pin the sticks in the middle to form a cross. Balance the sides by experimenting with the length of the string.

Tiger Shark

Loggerhead Sea Turtle

Plankton

Conch

Manta Ray

Coho Salmon

## Commensals

These little fish are **commensals**. Commensals means "those who eat at the same table." Some, such as the ramoras attach themselves to sharks with a suction disk on the tops of their heads. Others, such as pilot fish, swim free, sharing the scattered morsels of food from the sharks.

Sharksucker

Pilot Fish          Remora          Banded Rudderfish

## Threat Posture

Before an attack, the grey reef shark performs an exaggerated swimming display. This includes swimming with jerky movements, back arching, raising its snout and lowering its pectoral fins. When up close, it will swim in figure-8 loops. If this threat posture is ignored, the shark will attack.

Great White Shark

Southern Sting Ray

Sea Lion

Hammerhead Shark

Bull Shark

Horseshoe Crab

# Filter Feeders

Plankton are very tiny organisms which drift in the open water. **Phytoplankton** are tiny drifting plants and **zooplankton** are tiny drifting animals.

Whale sharks (the worlds largest living fish), basking sharks (the worlds second largest living fish) and megamouth sharks (first discovered in 1976) eat plankton. As water passes into the mouth and through the gills, the plankton are caught on filters. Sharks that eat plankton are **filter feeders**. On occasion they may eat small fish like sardines. Manta rays and other devil rays feed primarily on plankton. They have special **cephalic fins** on either side of their mouths to help channel water with plankton into their mouths.

One basking shark was found with 1000 pounds (453 kg) of plankton in its stomach. The shark probably did not eat this all in one day. How many hamburgers would this be? A hamburger from a fast food restaurant weighs about 1/4 pounds or 113 grams.

Basking Shark

Whale Shark

Manta Ray

Megamouth Shark

Plankton

## Slow Digestive Tracts

A shark's digestive tract works very slowly. It can take four days to digest a meal. This may be why sharks take 15 years or longer to grow to maturity and why they grow even more slowly during the rest of their life.

# Nurseries and Hiding Places

The ocean, like the land, offers many different habitats. In tropical and subtropical areas, mangrove forests are found along the coast. They provide important nursery areas for young sharks. The stilt-like roots, growing in the salt water, provide good hiding places. Animals, such as snails, live on the prop roots.

Lemon sharks give birth to live pups in the meadows of sea grasses that grow close-by. The pups live there for a few years traveling between the grasses and the roots until they are old enough to swim out to the open ocean.

Food is plentiful in this eat or be eaten world. Sharks feed on blue crabs and fish, such as yellowfin mojara and snappers. Big fish eat smaller fish, such as silversides and anchovies. Everyone looks out for barracudas. The yellowfin mojara extracts its food from the sand. It has to watch out for a buried southern stingray. Eagle rays swim by searching for conchs and clams. Ghost shrimp escape predators by living in borrows in the sand. Parrot fish, conchs, clams, sea stars and crabs eat the sea grass. Birds, nesting in the mangrove branches, swoop down to catch fish and shellfish.

**Study the picture and decide where you might find the following:**
(More than one number can go in a blank.)

\_\_\_\_\_ Where lemon sharks give birth
\_\_\_\_\_ Barracuda food
\_\_\_\_\_ Hiding place for young sharks
\_\_\_\_\_ Resting place for snails
\_\_\_\_\_ Resting place for conchs
\_\_\_\_\_ Nest site for birds
\_\_\_\_\_ Home for ghost shrimp
\_\_\_\_\_ Parrot fish food
\_\_\_\_\_ Food for conchs
\_\_\_\_\_ Hiding place for small fish
\_\_\_\_\_ Resting places for birds
\_\_\_\_\_ Yellowfin mojara food
\_\_\_\_\_ Lemon shark food
\_\_\_\_\_ Hiding place for stingrays.
\_\_\_\_\_ Spotted eagle ray food

Answers on last page

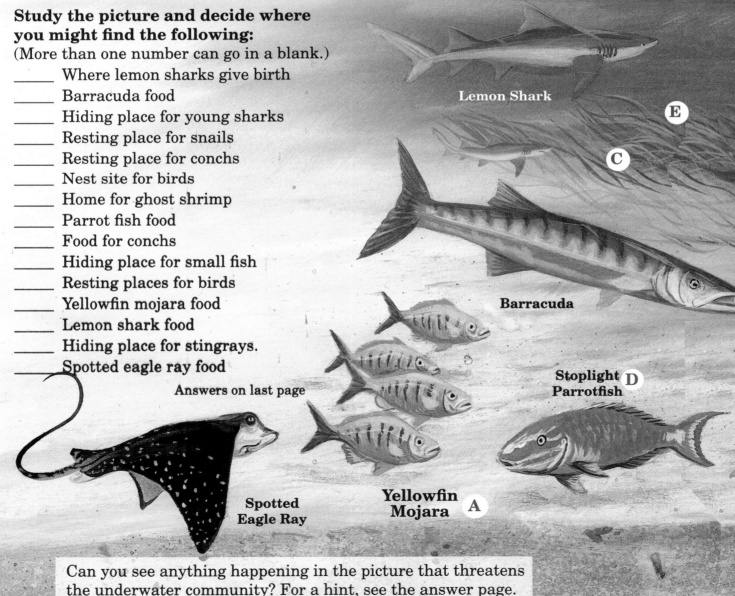

Lemon Shark

Barracuda

Stoplight Parrotfish

Spotted Eagle Ray

Yellowfin Mojara

Can you see anything happening in the picture that threatens the underwater community? For a hint, see the answer page.

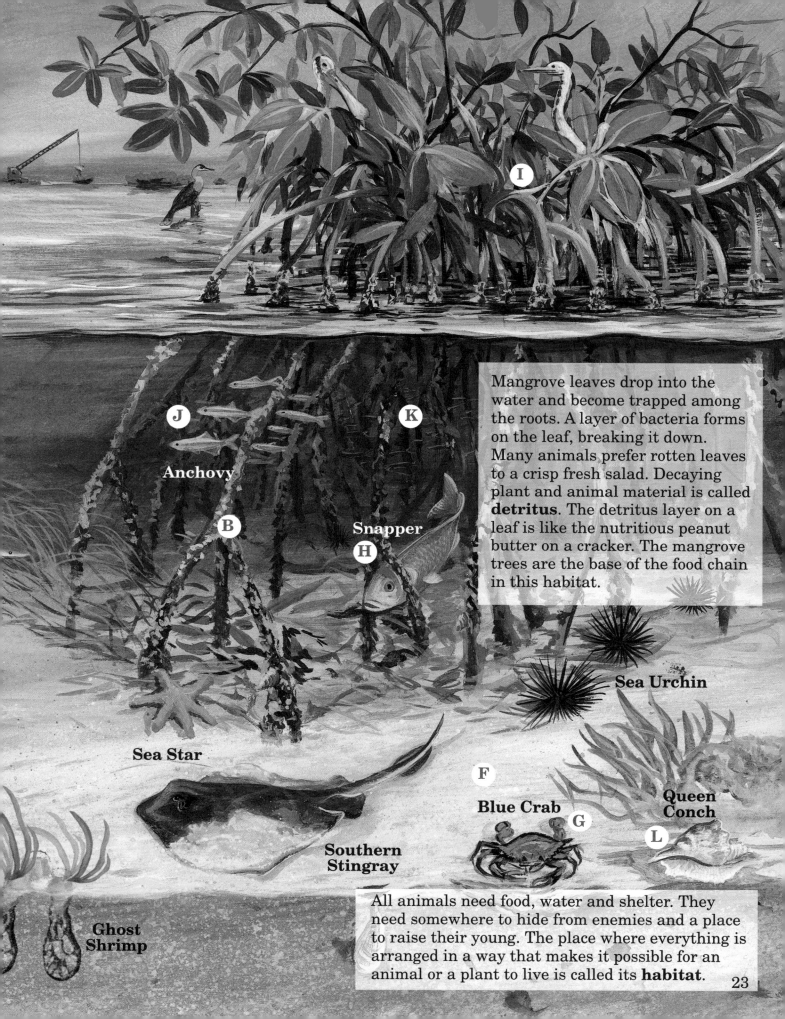

**I**

**J** **K**

**Anchovy**

Mangrove leaves drop into the water and become trapped among the roots. A layer of bacteria forms on the leaf, breaking it down. Many animals prefer rotten leaves to a crisp fresh salad. Decaying plant and animal material is called **detritus**. The detritus layer on a leaf is like the nutritious peanut butter on a cracker. The mangrove trees are the base of the food chain in this habitat.

**B**

**Snapper**
**H**

**Sea Urchin**

**Sea Star**

**F**

**Blue Crab**
**G**

**Queen Conch**

**Southern Stingray**

**L**

**Ghost Shrimp**

All animals need food, water and shelter. They need somewhere to hide from enemies and a place to raise their young. The place where everything is arranged in a way that makes it possible for an animal or a plant to live is called its **habitat**.

23

# Hiding In A Coral Reef

These sharks are hiding out in a coral reef—a colorful maze of canyons, caves, and castles. The coral reef is formed from the skeletons of tiny living and dead animals. A reef serves as a place for fish to feed and hide, and as a nursery for their babies. The special features that help sharks survive in their ocean habitat are known as adaptations. These include body shape, color, and even behavior.

**Find the following adaptations that help these sharks and rays survive in a coral reef and the nearby sandy shallows.** There may be more than one animal for each adaptation.

A. **Countershading**—darker on top and lighter on the belly. From above the animal appears dark like the ocean depths. From below it is like the light, shimmering water overhead.

B. **Submarine-shaped body**—helps shark swim safely through the water

C. **Splotchy markings**—camouflage fish, helping it blend with rocks, coral, and seaweed

D. **Flattened** with broad, fin like wings —allows the animal to hide under a layer of sand.

E. **Wide hammer-shaped head**— may provide lift when swimming. Special sensing organs may help detect food under the sand.

F. **Stinging spines** on top of tail— provide defense against enemies

G. **Tail Shape** —the tail (almost as long as the body) can be used to herd other smaller fish and squid for dinner.

H. **Hiding Behavior**—during the day many fish hide in crack, crevices and coral caves where they are safe from larger predators.

### Pinning the Prey

A hammerhead's strange shaped head may help it find one of its favorite meals—a ray buried in the sand. Its long head has extra ampullae of Lorenzini that can sense electrical fields. When the shark catches a ray, it can pin it down with the edge of its head and then eat it.

Galapagos Shark

Whitetip Reef Shark

Thrasher Shark- out
deeper in the ocean

Tiger Shark

Scalloped
Hammerhead
Shark

Blacktip
Reef Shark

Smooth
Hammerhead
Shark

Brown Stingray

# Pups and Purses

A shark's life cycle starts with an egg that has been fertilized by the sperm of a male shark.

Sharks and rays begin their lives in one of three ways:

1. Some are nourished and develop inside their mother's body. Babies, or **pups**, are born live, just like human babies. Pups all born at the same time to one mother are members of a **litter**.

2. Some pups hatch from eggs laid in the ocean. The animal grows by feeding on the yolk in the egg. These eggs are not smooth and rounded like chicken eggs. Instead they have a thick, tough, rubbery or leathery case that blends in with the surroundings. Egg cases have different shapes. Some look like sacks and are called **mermaids' purses**. Others are spiral-shaped. Mother sharks use their mouths to wedge the soft spiral cases into rock crevices where they harden. All have threadlike tendrils to anchor them in one place.

3. Pups may also hatch from egg cases that stay inside the mother's body. The mother's body provides a safe place for the eggs until they are ready to hatch. Then they are born into the sea.

Pups are small versions of their parents. No adult looks after them. They are good swimmers and begin to feed almost immediately.

Two young researchers have donned their scuba diving gear and are exploring a kelp forest. **Can you help them name the sharks they meet? Use the clues from the table on the next page? Write the letter of the shark next to its name in the table.**

Mermaid's Purse Egg Case

Spiral Egg Case

**Shark - Egg Case or Pup**

____ Angelshark
    Soft egg case inside mother

____ Blue Shark
    Pup

____ California Hornshark
    Screw-shaped egg case

____ Leopard Shark
    Soft egg case inside mother

____ Port Jackson Shark
    Screw-shaped egg case

____ Swellshark
    Purse -
    Green-amber colored)

____ Bat Ray
    Soft egg case inside mother

**Extra Clues**

Flattened, kite-shaped shark.

Slender, blue shark; Live birth, born tail first.

Small dark spots on bodies. Spines in front of dorsal fins.

Black spots and saddle shaped markings on slender body.

Harness-like markings on body of adult.

Adult has brown blotches on yellow to brown background, small dorsal fins.

Broad disk with rounded snout. Dark brown to black on top.

E

G Inset - A
Shark from
Australia

F

27

# Risk Taking

Why are sharks in trouble? They've been around for millions of years. They survived when the dinosaurs didn't. The ocean is huge, so they have plenty of space.

Some of their problem is due to their **birth rate**—how many babies a mother has in any one year and how old she is when she starts having babies.

**Bony fish** have a **high birth rate**. The females lay lots of eggs—thousands or even millions of eggs. Females often produce eggs by the time they are 2 or 3 years old. Many of these eggs are not fertilized. They do not grow. Parent fish cannot look after their thousands of babies. The tiny fish have to fend for themselves. They may not be able to find their own food. Or they may end up as someone else's dinner. Some die from poor water conditions and some from disease. It is good to have a high birth rate so that enough babies grow up to keep the species going, even in difficult years.

Sharks and rays have a **low birth rate**. They have only a few offspring. They are also very slow to mature. Most females do not have pups until they are 7 or 8 years old. Some are 20 years old. Mostly they give birth only every other year. The mother is pregnant from 9 to 24 months, depending on the species. Often there are only 1 to 10 pups in a litter. Some have as many as 100 eggs or pups. But that is not much compared with bony fish with their millions of eggs.

Because pups are bigger they have a better chance of growing up. The population remains steady if only two pups survive to replace their parents.

A low birth rate works well for top predators. In healthy, safe waters, many pups live. But in bad years, the numbers drop. It takes a long time to recover. Sharks can't afford to have a bad year.

How long do sharks and rays live? Most live 20 to 30 years. Spiny dogfish can live to be 100. Whale sharks live about 60 years.

# Staying Alive

Will your shark or ray population survive? Your luck depends on how many pups you have and how often you have them. It also depends on whether or not you have one or more bad years.

**Game**: You start out with a group of 10 sharks or rays—5 females and 5 males. You are a winner if you have 10 or more animals alive at the end of the game. The outcome depends on which path you follow. You may land on a trouble-free path that is like a shark's life in the past. Or you may land on a dangerous path like a shark's life today.

**You will need**:
- Four objects (paper or pebbles) numbered 1,2,3, and 4. A die works if you ignore 5 and 6.
- Pencil and paper to keep track of your population.
- A playing piece. Decide if you are a shark or ray. You can use a shark or ray sticker on a firm backing, or, use a pebble or a coin. You could trace one of these sharks or rays, color it, cut it out, and tape it to a penny. Your playing piece stands for a population of 10 pups.
- You also need the game board on the next page.

**Great White Shark**

**Tiger Shark**

**Hammerhead Shark**

**Eagle Ray**

**Directions**:
1. Place your playing piece on START. Decide who goes first.
2. Draw a number and move your playing piece, following the instructions on the board. Keep track of the animals lost or gained along the way.
3. Watch for places where each player must stop. You do not have to draw an exact number to stop at "All Stop."
4. Feeding Stations. Not all sharks eat the same thing. See shark's menu on the right.
5. Birth Stations. All players must land on first birth station. By the time you reach this stop, all your sharks are adults. Follow directions to figure out number of pups born. In this game, 4 pups are born per pair. In nature, they may have fewer or more babies.
6. If you end the game with 10 or more animals, your population will survive, and you are a winner.
7. What did you learn from playing this game?
   Does it matter how many babies are born at one time?
   Does it matter if babies are born every year?
   What problems do humans cause for sharks and rays?

## Menu

*White Shark Choices*
Seals, sea lions, dolphins, whales, fish, other sharks

*Tiger Shark Choices*
Seals, sea lions, sea turtles, eagle rays, dolphins, whales, sea snakes, birds

*Hammerhead Choices*
Eagle rays, other rays, fish

*Eagle Ray Choices*
Oysters, clams, snails, octopus, shrimp, fish

**Actual Pups in Litters**
Great White - 4 to 9, Tiger - 10 to 82, Hammerhead - 20 to 40, Eagle Ray - 1 to 4

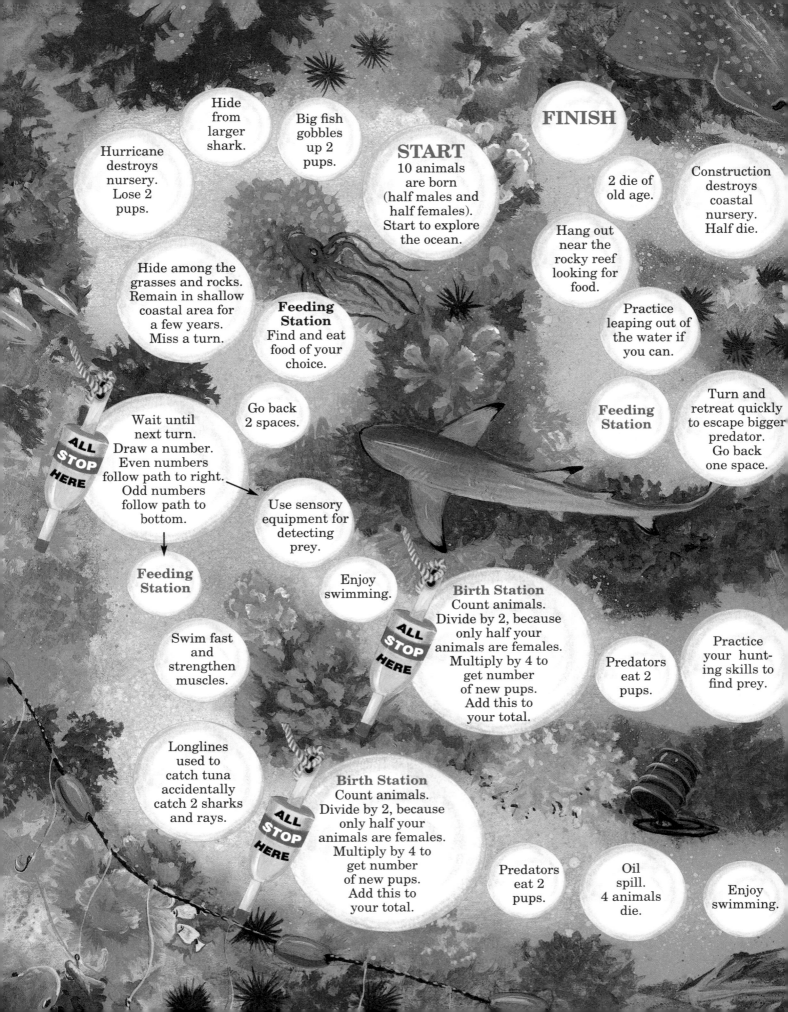

In trouble because of over fishing. Lose half of your animals.

**Birth Station** Follow directions from first station.

**Bycatch** Caught accidentally . 4 discarded at sea.

Pollution such as sewage causes 6 to die.

Swim quickly around discarded plastic. Don't get caught.

**Sharks Only** 6 sharks die from finning. Fins are used to make soup.

**Birth Station** Follow directions from first station.

**Feeding Station**

Swim fast and strengthen muscles.

4 caught and die in beach meshing used to protect swimming beaches.

Search for food.

Cyclone damages nursery habitat. Lose 8 animals.

Predators feast on 2 pups.

Admired by scuba divers.

Anglers catch 2 as trophy fish.

**Cleaning Station** Small fish help clean mouth and other openings.

Released by scientists who are tagging sharks. Swim ahead 4 spaces.

Hungry island people catch 2 animals to use for food and other products.

**Feeding Station**

Predators eat 2 pups.

Sail through the open ocean.

**Birth Station** Follow directions from first station.

Coastal farming of shrimp contaminates water with disease Lose 4.

**Feeding Station**

Illegal fishing catches 2 animals in marine protected reserve.

**Birth Station** Follow directions from first station.

Predators eat 2 pups.

Drift nets used to catch tuna and squid accidentally catch 4 sharks and rays.

# Why Are Sharks In Trouble?

As you have learned by reading this book and playing the game, there are many problems for sharks. Use the secret code to fill in the boxes below with the correct letter. You will find many of the problems sharks and rays face.

| 1 | 2 | 3 | 4 | 5 | 6 | 7 | 8 | 9 | 10 | 11 | 12 | 13 | 14 | 15 | 16 | 17 | 18 | 19 | 20 | 21 | 22 | 23 | 24 | 25 | 26 |
|---|---|---|---|---|---|---|---|---|---|---|---|---|---|---|---|---|---|---|---|---|---|---|---|---|---|
| A | B | C | D | E | F | G | H | I | J | K | L | M | N | O | P | Q | R | S | T | U | V | W | X | Y | Z |

**A.** __ __ __ __  __ __ __ __ __ __ __
15 22 5 18  6 9 19 8 9 14 7

Taking more fish than can be replaced by births is called _____. In recent years, as many as 12 to 100 million sharks are killed in one year.

**B.** __ __ __ __ __ __ __ __
2 25 3 1 20 3 8

Commercial fishermen fish for business. Recreational fishermen fish for sport and enjoyment. Both types of fishermen accidentally catch sharks and rays by mistake.

**C.** __ __ __ __ __ __ __ __ __ __ __
8 1 9 2 22 1 20 12 15 19 19

When a wild place is lost or changed, it is often unsuitable for the plants and animals that once lived there. Some changes are natural, like hurricanes. Other changes are human-caused, like dredging for harbors or clearing for buildings.

**D.** __ __ __ __ __ __ __ __ __
16 15 12 12 21 20 9 15 14

Some materials are dangerous to plants and animals. Oil spills, other chemicals, plastic garbage, and acid rain spell big trouble for ocean life.

**E.** __ __ __ __ __ __ __
6 9 14 14 9 14 7

Slicing off a shark's fin and throwing the rest of the body in the ocean is called _____. Cut off fins are dried and made into shark fin soup. In 2000, the United States passed a law banning this wasteful practice in all U.S. waters. But most waters are not protected, and sharks are still finned all over the world.

**F.** __ __ __ __
14 5 20 19

_____ of all sorts are serious threats. From those set out to protect beaches, to drift nets, trawl nets, seine nets and gillnets used for fishing, sharks and rays get tangled and die.

**G.** __ __ __ __ __ __  __ __ __ __ __ __ __ __
7 12 15 2 1 12  23 1 18 13 9 14 7

Scientists are discussing if the earth is getting warmer. Climate changes will affect sharks. If the sea level changes and water temperatures go up, the habitat for sharks and rays is changed.

# Safety in Shark Territory

Few sharks attack people. Among the most dangerous are the great white, the tiger, the bull, and the oceanic whitetip sharks, but other species do sometimes attack people. Even so, you are more likely to be struck by lightning than to be killed by a shark. Recently there were 43,500 auto deaths, 63 lightning deaths, 46 bee-sting deaths in the US in a single year. Worldwide, 6 people were killed by sharks in 2010 and 17 people killed by sharks in 2011.

However, people swimming in shark waters must be cautious. To a shark, swimmers and surfers look like their favorite food—seals or turtles.

Look at the situations below. Write "safe" or "unsafe" below each picture. Talk with others about your answer. If you aren't sure, check safety ideas on page 40.

**Beware - Don't Look Like Shark Food**

Seal     Person on Surfboard

---

| Let's swim together here. Don't worry, that is a small shark | Sharks won't see us This water is cloudy. | I think I'll go for an early morning swim. | This is just a little cut. It shouldn't matter if I swim. |
|---|---|---|---|

---

| Sharks Seen. Do Not Swim. | Oops! I fell in the water. I better take off my clothes and shoes. | | I'm going to defend myself against this shark attack. |
|---|---|---|---|

---

| Diver using regulator blows bubbles into shark face. | Let's huddle together so we don't look like shark food. | Researchers try repellents like electric signals to repel sharks without harming them. | Researchers try out special scuba diving suits made from materials like stainless-steel chain-mail. |
|---|---|---|---|

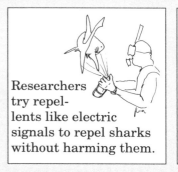

# Studying Sharks

Sharks and rays are mysterious creatures. We still have a lot to learn. To learn about how sharks really live, researchers need to study them in the wild. They bring their results back to their labs to continue their research. Scientists look for answers to questions like these.

How much and what do sharks eat?

Where do sharks breed?

Where and when do they travel?

How long do they live?

Are sharks important to the way ecosystems work?

Do sharks cooperate when they hunt?

Do they communicate with each other?

Are sharks and rays dying? Why?

How can humans be safe in shark waters?

How can sharks be safe?

The answers help us understand the life of each kind of shark and ray, how they interact with fellow creatures in the ocean. It helps us know if they are currently safe or if they are in trouble.

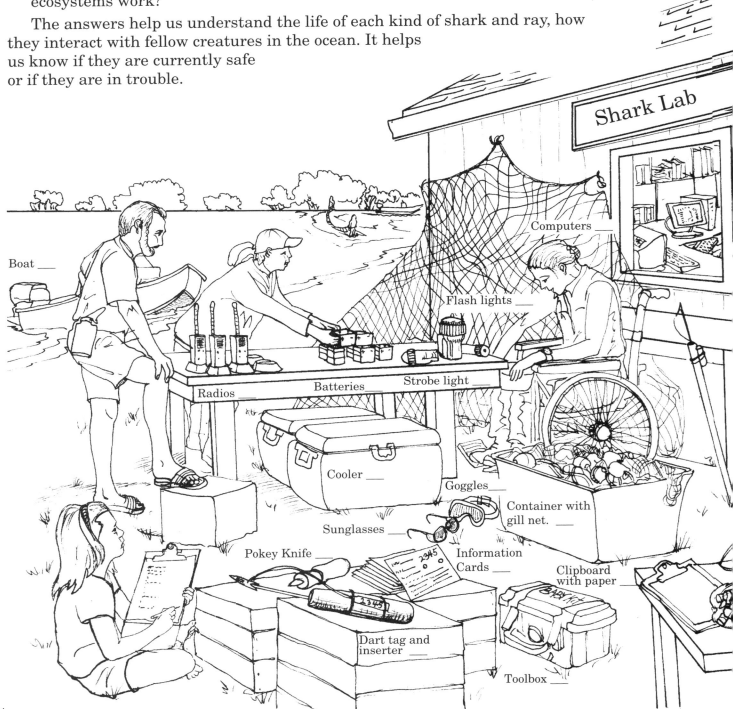

Shark Lab

Boat ___

Computers ___

Flash lights ___

Radios ___

Batteries ___

Strobe light ___

Cooler ___

Goggles ___

Sunglasses ___

Container with gill net. ___

Pokey Knife ___

Information Cards ___

Clipboard with paper ___

Dart tag and inserter ___

Toolbox ___

The scientists are preparing to tag sharks. They must be very careful, because they are going to do their work overnight. They are checking out their equipment.

**Can you match each type of equipment with its correct job?**

A. Keeps human bodies warm in cold water.

B. Blinking light used to see things in the dark, e.g. boats, channels in the water.

C. Large bright light used to signal.

D. Picks up ultrasonic sounds and locates sharks.

E. Used to locate sharks from water. It picks up signals from the shark's transmitter.

F. Placed on tails of sharks recovering from problem so scientists can watch and see if they are well.

G. Draws blood samples for tests.

H. Place to record information.

I. Placed on shark for future identification.

J. Used to capture smaller sharks.

K. Used to communicate with each other.

L. Bounces signal off a PIT tag and reads a number.

M. Carries food and keep things, such as clothes, dry.

N. Keep people dry in the boats.

O. Gear used on face to protect eyes and breath while in water.

P. Backup power for radios and lights.

Q. Medical aid.

R. Used to protect samples.

S. Filled with saline, a protective sterile solution, to carry samples, like DNA from fins, back to a lab.

T. Electronic equipment to store and analyze data.

U. Punches out a sample, e.g. from the fin, to use for DNA testing.

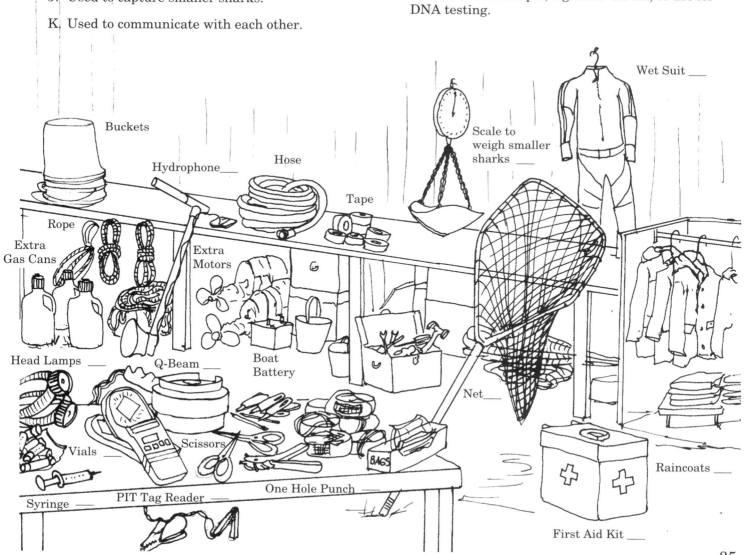

Buckets

Hydrophone___

Hose

Tape

Scale to weigh smaller sharks ___

Wet Suit ___

Rope

Extra Gas Cans

Extra Motors

Head Lamps ___

Q-Beam ___

Boat Battery

Net___

Vials ___

Scissors___

BAGS

Raincoats ___

Syringe ___

PIT Tag Reader ___

One Hole Punch ___

First Aid Kit ___

# Be a Shark Biologist

Scientists have just captured a shark in a shallow bay. Help them weigh, measure and tag it. **Tagging** is placing a tracking device on an animal in order to follow its movements and behavior over time. Here they are using a kind of tag called a PIT tag that is placed just below the dorsal fin. It is about the size of a grain of rice. PIT stands for Passive Integrated Transponder. A tiny incision is made with a scalpel, and the pit tag is placed inside the opening. The wound will heal in a short time. Each tag has its own number inside a tiny capsule. The number can be read with a PIT tag reader, which sends out a microwave that bounces off the tag and its number is read.

Fill in information on the clip board below. Use the shark on the scale to get facts, or **data**. Record your conclusions.

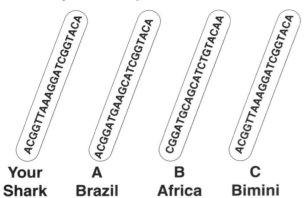

## Be a DNA Detective

In the lab, the fin sample is processed and the DNA is extracted. Scientists can tell from the DNA if sharks are related. They are trying to find out if they return to their birthplace to reproduce and if they migrate across oceans.

**PIT Tag Reader**

The following diagram shows parts of a strand of DNA from your shark and from other sharks. Look at the code along its length. Which shark is most closely related to yours?

**Your Shark** — ACGGTTAAAGGATCGGTACA

**A Brazil** — ACGGATGAAGCATCGGTACA

**B Africa** — CGGATGCAGCATCTGTACAA

**C Bimini** — ACGGTTAAAGGATCGGTACA

1. Kind of shark_____
   *Hint: The two dorsal fins are about the same size.*

2. Weight _____pounds or _____kg
   *Hint: 1 kilogram (kg) equals about 2.2 pounds*

3. Length _____inches or _____cm
   *Hint: 1 centimeter (cm) equals .3937 inches*

4. Put a mark just below the dorsal fin where the PIT tag will be inserted to mark the spot. It will be about 1/4 of an inch deep.

5. Tag Number_____
   (Give the tag a unique number that will identify the shark all its life. The tags are actually purchased with a number already on each tag.)

6. Mark a spot on the left pectoral fin where you will take a fin sample for DNA tests.

7. Your shark DNA matches sample _____.

## Tagging and Tracking Sharks

The movements of sharks can be tracked with different kinds of equipment, depending on the type of tag placed on the shark. Scientists might use hydrophones in the water and satellites from the skies.

# Chew On A Puzzle

Sink your teeth into solving this crossword puzzle. Write each word in the space next to the definition. You will have made both a glossary and an index.

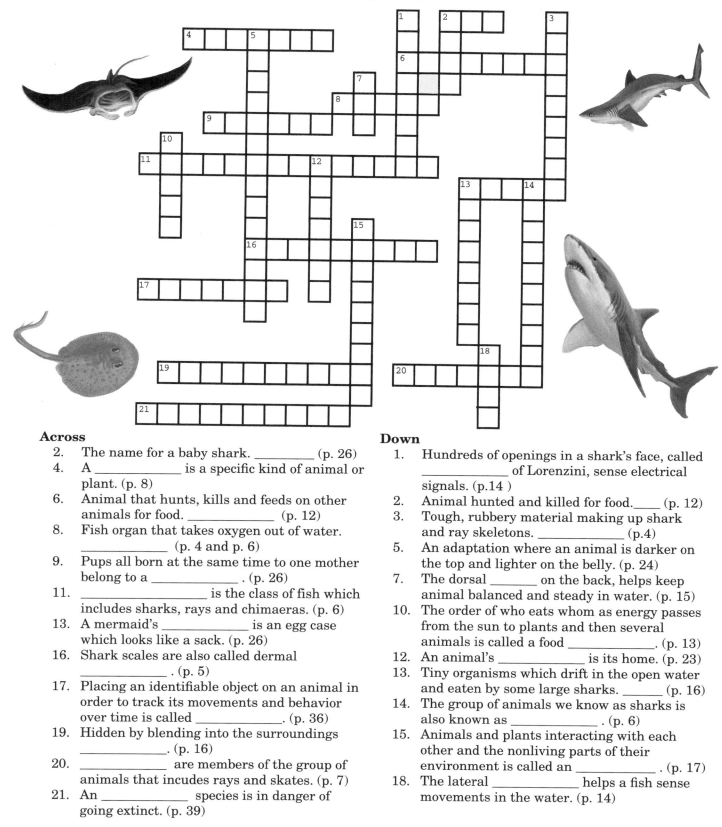

## Across

2. The name for a baby shark. _____ (p. 26)
4. A _____ is a specific kind of animal or plant. (p. 8)
6. Animal that hunts, kills and feeds on other animals for food. _____ (p. 12)
8. Fish organ that takes oxygen out of water. _____ (p. 4 and p. 6)
9. Pups all born at the same time to one mother belong to a _____ . (p. 26)
11. _____ is the class of fish which includes sharks, rays and chimaeras. (p. 6)
13. A mermaid's _____ is an egg case which looks like a sack. (p. 26)
16. Shark scales are also called dermal _____ . (p. 5)
17. Placing an identifiable object on an animal in order to track its movements and behavior over time is called _____. (p. 36)
19. Hidden by blending into the surroundings _____. (p. 16)
20. _____ are members of the group of animals that incudes rays and skates. (p. 7)
21. An _____ species is in danger of going extinct. (p. 39)

## Down

1. Hundreds of openings in a shark's face, called _____ of Lorenzini, sense electrical signals. (p.14 )
2. Animal hunted and killed for food.____ (p. 12)
3. Tough, rubbery material making up shark and ray skeletons. _____ (p.4)
5. An adaptation where an animal is darker on the top and lighter on the belly. (p. 24)
7. The dorsal _____ on the back, helps keep animal balanced and steady in water. (p. 15)
10. The order of who eats whom as energy passes from the sun to plants and then several animals is called a food _____. (p. 13)
12. An animal's _____ is its home. (p. 23)
13. Tiny organisms which drift in the open water and eaten by some large sharks. _____ (p. 16)
14. The group of animals we know as sharks is also known as _____ . (p. 6)
15. Animals and plants interacting with each other and the nonliving parts of their environment is called an _____ . (p. 17)
18. The lateral _____ helps a fish sense movements in the water. (p. 14)

# Protection Worldwide

It is hard to believe that the animal that people fear the most now needs our protection. People are far more dangerous to sharks than sharks are to people! When too many of any one species is killed, it is hard for a population to recover. That species may become endangered.

Some nations are setting aside protected waters as parks, reserves or sanctuaries. Although the area may be set aside for only one kind of animal, such as a whale, it becomes a safe area for other marine life. Protection rules vary from place to place. Activities, such as dumping, drilling, and dredging, may be prohibited. Many areas do not allow fishing or other harvesting. It is often hard to enforce rules, especially in remote areas.

You have been given the job of reporting back on existing and possible sanctuaries. Travel the world maze and visit each site without retracing your path. Notice the symbol at each site. Find its matching symbol and learn about the area.

**START**

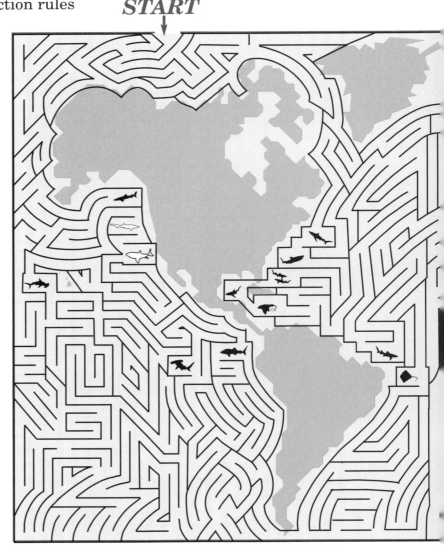

 **Gwaii Haanas National Marine Conservation Area** A proposed Canadian area provides habitat for spiny dogfish.

 **Olympic Coast National Marine Sanctuary** About 14 kinds of sharks and rays live here. There are restrictions on fishing for the sevengill shark.

 **Several Sanctuaries on California Coast** Channel Islands, Cordell Bank, Gulf of the Farallones, and Monterey Bay provide habitat and nutrient rich waters for sharks like great whites.

 **Hawaiian Islands Humpback Whale Sanctuary** The sanctuary safeguards numerous sharks and rays such as scalloped hammerheads.

 **Gorgona Island National Park** Reef sharks and whale sharks live here. The park tries to protect sharks from finning.

 **Galapagos Islands** Law officers struggle to protect great hammerheads and others from illegal fishing.

 **Parque Nacional Fernando De Noronha** Established to protect birds, this park off the coast of Brazil shelters southern stingray and nurse sharks.

 **Atol das Rocas** is a haven for lemon sharks.

 **Bimini, Bahama Islands** (not an official sanctuary) The shallow bays provide some of the best nurseries for lemon sharks and deserves protection.

 **Flower Garden Banks** Coral reefs protect Caribbean reef sharks.

 **Florida Keys National Marine Sanctuary** Mangrove shores, sea grasses and coral reefs provide a range of habitats for sharks and rays, such as spotted eagle rays.

 **Grays Reef National Marine Sanctuary** Many sharks like the tiger find some protection.

**Stellwagen Bank National Marine Sanctuary** This important sanctuary for whales also has blue sharks.

 **United Kingdom** With 20,000 tons of sharks caught yearly and worry about dogfish landings, this area is an excellent candidate for protection.

**Banc D'Arguin National Park** The reserve struggles to control illegal fishing. Sawfishes have disappeared. Guitarfish are common.

 **Mediterranean Whale Sanctuary** Haven for sharks such as great whites and angelsharks.

 **Dyer Island** A reserve around the island protects great white sharks.

 **East Coast of India** With up to 55,000 tons of sharks fished yearly, it is a candidate for protection.

 **Philippine Islands** Whale shark fishing has been prohibited.

 **New Zealand** Sixteen reserves help protect several sharks such as carpet and basking sharks.

**Australia** Numerous sanctuaries try to protect many such as nurse and great white sharks.

*Where one kind of shark is protected, others have a better chance to survive.*

## Sustainable Fishing

**Sustainable fishing** means keeping a balance between the number of fish born and the number dying and being caught. In a healthy fish population, we can catch fish, but still leave enough to produce the next generation. When we **overfish**, we catch too many, and the numbers drop. The population may not recover or recovery may take a long time. We need to figure out a way to fish that will help sharks stay healthy and allow future people to catch fish, too.

## Aquariums and Education

Public aquariums play an important role in protecting sharks. Through well designed displays and educational programs, they help people understand sharks and their role they play in their environment. Knowledge reduces fears and myths that surround these animals. Education is essential!

You, too, can educate others about the lives of sharks and the threats they face. Learn and talk to others about their importance in the world's oceans.

# Answers

p. 4    A-Bony fish, B-Shark

p. 8    Whale Shark - Tropical, Subtropical; Great White Shark - Tropical, Subtropical, Temperate; Scalloped Hammerhead - Tropical, Subtropical; Mako Shark - Tropical, Subtropical, Temperate; Southern Stingray - Subtropical, Temperate; Porbeagle Shark - Subtropical, Temperate; Salmon Shark - Temperate, Polar; Greenland Shark - Polar

p. 15    A-3; B-1; C-3

p. 16    1. Jump out of water; 2. Lie on beach; 3. Swim zig-zag; 4. Fly away; 5. Hide; 6. Camouflage (blend into surroundings); 7. Electric Shock; 8. Swim in schools; 9. Dig into sand

p. 17    Pattern for Ocean Mobile

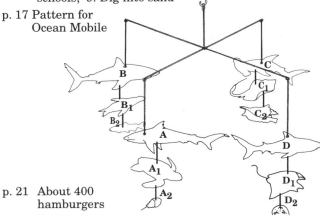

p. 21    About 400 hamburgers

p. 22    Notice the dredge on the top left of page 23. People may destroy shorelines for other purposes, such as buildings. Where will the sharks have their pups if their habitat is destroyed?

| | | | |
|---|---|---|---|
| E | Shark birth | E | Conch food |
| A,C,D,H,J | Barracuda food | E,K | Hiding place |
| | | I | Resting Place |
| E,K | Hiding place | F | Mojara food |
| B,F | Resting Snails | I | Perch |
| F | Resting Conchs | A,D,J | Lemon shark food |
| I | Nest site | F | Hiding stingray |
| F | Home shrimp | L | Food eagle ray |
| E | Parrotfish food | | |

p. 24    A. Countershading—Tiger, Hammerhead, Blacktip, Galapagos, Whitetip;  B. Sub-marine-shaped body —Tiger, Blacktip, Galapagos, Whitetip;  C. Splotchy markings —Tiger; D. Flattened—Brown Stingray; E. Wide hammer-shaped head—Smooth Hammer head; F. Stinging Spines—Brown Stingray; G. Tail Shape—Thrasher; H. Hiding Behavior—Whitetip Reef, Brown Stingray

p. 27    Pups - F-Angelshark; E-Blue Shark; D-California Hornshark; A-Leopard Shark; G-Port Jackson Shark; C-Swellshark; B-Bat Ray

p. 32    A. Overfishing; B. Bycatch; C. Habitat Loss; D. Pollution; E. Finning; F. Nets; G. Global Warming

p. 34    Studying Sharks

| | | |
|---|---|---|
| A. Wet Suit | I. Dart Tag and Container | O. Snorkel/Mask |
| B. Strobe Light | | P. Batteries |
| C. Q-Beam | J. Net | Q. First Aid Kit |
| D. Hydrophone | K. Radios | R. Plastic bags |
| E. Boat | L. Pit Tag Reader | S. Vials |
| F. Tail Tags | | T. Computers |
| G. Syringe | M. Cooler | U. One Hole Puncher |
| H. Clipboard | N. Rain Coats | |

## p. 33 Safety in Shark Territory

1. Swim with a buddy. Don't swim with a shark, no matter how small. Trained scuba divers may dive with some sharks, but most people should not.

2. Sharks don't have to see you to find you.

3. Many sharks feed at night and into the early morning hours.

4. Sharks are attracted to blood, even from far away.

5. If sharks have been seen in the area, don't swim.

6. Clothes may protect you from a shark attack. If a shark rubs against you, you would not feel like prey. Also, a shark rubbing against your bare skin might cause you to bleed, provoking an attack.

7. Stay calm. Irregular movements made in panic can attract sharks.

8. Be strong and try to defend yourself. Hit the shark on the nose. Stick fingers or anything else in its eyes, nostrils or gills.

9. Scuba divers can turn their regulators and blow bubbles toward the shark.

10. Change the position of your body so you do not look like shark food. Float in a crouching position. Huddle together with others forming a circle. These shapes might help prevent shark attacks.

p. 36    Shark Biologist 1. Lemon shark;  2. 4 pounds; 1.8 kg;  3. 22 inches; 55.8 cm; 7. Your shark matches C

p. 37    Crossword

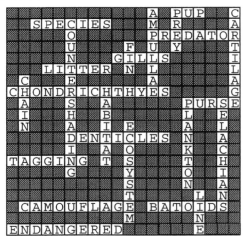

p. 38 Protection

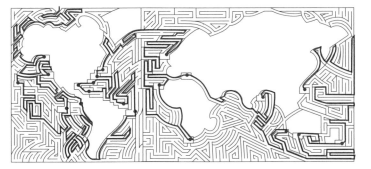